Happy Birthday!

A song that will work its way into your heart and your family's traditions!

Copyright 2017 by Philip M. Hudson.
The book author retains sole copyright
to his contributions to this book.

Published 2017.
Printed in the United States of America.

All rights reserved.

No portion of this book may be reproduced, stored in a retrieval system, or transmitted in any form or by any means – electronic, mechanical, photocopy, recording, scanning, or other – except for brief quotations in critical reviews or articles, without the prior written permission of the author.

ISBN 978-1-943650-63-7

Library of Congress Control Number 2017954700

Illustrations – Google Images.

This book may be ordered from online bookstores.

Published by BookCrafters Parker, Colorado.
www.bookcrafters.net

Have a Happy Birthday!

"Happy Birthday to You"
dates to the 1890s. It is one
of the most recognizable songs
in the English language. However,
this book isn't about that traditional
rendition. Instead, it celebrates a new
way to commemorate the anniversaries
of our births. Only time will tell if
these refreshing lines and this
catchy tune will capture
the number one spot
in our hearts.

Happy birthday!

Have a.....happy birthday!

This is your day,

to have a lot of fun! O well a.....

We're all waiting for the…..celebration,

for the celebration to begin! B...B...B...

Blow out the candles on the cake and make a wish!

Serve everybody's favorite dish.....

favorite dish, O well a,

Happy birthday.....

Have a.....happy birthday!

This is your day!

So happy birthday to you!!

Singing together
is fun.

(Has your family memorized
the song, yet?)

Compiled by Phil Hudson

Phil and Jan have been married for 50 years and have 7 children and over 20 grandchildren. They have been singing this song with their family for nearly half a century.

Happy Birthday!

www.ingramcontent.com/pod-product-compliance
Lightning Source LLC
Chambersburg PA
CBHW041229240426
43661CB00013B/1174